T0132022

A Whisper to A Child's Ear From God

Josh

© 2010 Josh. All rights reserved.

No part of this book may be reproduced, stored in a retrieval system, or transmitted by any means without the written permission of the author.

AuthorHouse™
1663 Liberty Drive
Bloomington, IN 47403
www.authorhouse.com
Phone: 833-262-8899

Because of the dynamic nature of the Internet, any web addresses or links contained in this book may have changed since publication and may no longer be valid. The views expressed in this work are solely those of the author and do not necessarily reflect the views of the publisher, and the publisher hereby disclaims any responsibility for them.

Any people depicted in stock imagery provided by Getty Images are models, and such images are being used for illustrative purposes only.
Certain stock imagery © Getty Images.

This book is printed on acid-free paper.

ISBN: 978-1-4490-7020-5 (sc)

Library of Congress Control Number: 2010900499

Print information available on the last page.

Published by AuthorHouse 01/10/2023

authorHOUSE®

Contents

Introduction

My name is Joshua Walker. I am twelve years old. I have something to share with you. I was born in Laguna Hills, California, on December 28, 1995. My mother told me that I was a good baby and that I never cried. My mother told me that when I was two years old, we were sitting outside and the phone rang. My mom went into the house to answer the telephone. When she came back, I was gone. My mother looked for me for fifteen minutes, running around in the complex. When she returned, I was sitting on the step, waiting for her like nothing ever happened or I never left. I have always been misunderstood and often taken advantage of; my mother always had to come to my rescue. For instance, when I was three years old at the daycare, the teacher said that I had bitten a little girl and that I would have to stay at home for two days. My mother asked the director to play the video tape for that room, and it showed another child biting the little girl. In another instance, when I was playing in the sandbox on the playground with my back toward a little girl, I was digging with a shovel. The sand came

1

up over my head, and it went into the little girl's eyes. The little girl went crying that I had thrown dirt in her eyes. I was written up for that, but then my mother stepped in and asked me to sit down on the floor in front of the teacher and show her what had happened. The teacher said, "Oh, he didn't mean to do it; it was an accident." These incidents always happened throughout my life. My mother said, "When you are a child of God, you will always be protected by God." I have always tried to do the right thing and stay focused. This book is a true story about my dreams and my life and how they affected me. My gift is hard to explain, but I get these whispers in my ear that come true. Because I have this power, I've connected more with God.

Third-grade Dream

When I was in third grade, I had a dream that my mother was at this place yelling my name, but I couldn't tell why she was yelling my name. I remember that we were sitting on the green grass, and there was water around us. I woke up from the dream, and my mother was running the vacuum cleaner. My mother asked me what was wrong. I told her that I'd had a dream that she was at a place where she was sitting on green grass and surrounded by water and that she was yelling my name. My mother asked whether she was yelling like she was happy or upset. I said, "Mother, you were scared. The next day, my mom was one of the parents to volunteer to be a chaperone at the Charleston, South Carolina, aquarium. My mother was responsible for me and another child. The dream came true; my mother lost my classmate and went yelling throughout the aquarium until she found him with another group of kids (my mother was so happy she found him). The class went outside of the aquarium for lunch and sat on the green grass, which was surrounded by water. The dream came true. The only thing different was that my mother was not yelling my name; she was yelling the other kid's name.

Staying Focus to Receive

Lots of people have dreams all the time. If you really believe in dreams, they will come true. My mother told me that if you truly, truly, believe in dreams and stay focused and continue praying to God, he will give you everything he thinks you need. Every night when I go to sleep, I pray and thank the Lord that we are financially blessed. You see, we are blessed that he keeps food on the table and clothes on my back. I am so glad that he is living in my heart. My goal is to stay focused and grow up to play in the NFL (I just love football). I dream of wealth all the time, but I don't know where it is or what it means. All I know is that if you truly believe in the Lord Jesus Christ, you will receive your blessing if you always put him first.

My Prayer to God and His Answer to Me

When I was in the third grade, I was struggling with reading. I had made all As and Bs in other subjects, but in reading I made a D on my last progress report. My teacher wanted to hold me back because she said that I would be in trouble when I got to the next grade. My teacher told my mother that she could not hold me back unless she signed the papers. I walked into the kitchen where my mother was sitting while thinking about whether or not she would sign the paper to have me repeat the third grade. I said to my mother, "Don't worry about it; I have already prayed about it." My mother asked me what I had prayed about. I told her that I had prayed to God, asking him for a B. When I received my report card on that last day, I received a B in reading, and I made the A and B honor roll and received six awards.

When I pray and ask God for anything within reason, he always comes through for me. (But if you ask God for a car, you may have to work for it.) I think that if you think positively and stay focused, God will lead the way and give you signs and always be there for you.

The Whisper to My Mother's Ear from Me

One day my mother was talking about a problem that she was having. My mother said that she was going to see a lawyer and that she would have to a pay a fee. I went with my mother. She was determined to solve this problem by going to a lawyer. Once we got to the lawyer's office, we sat in the car. I asked my mother if she was sure she had a good lawyer, because I had received a whisper in my ear that this lawyer was not going to help her. My mother and I went into the building. I could not convince my mother. She said, "Son, I know what I'm doing." When my mother came out, she was not too happy. I asked her what was wrong, and when she told me, I said, "Mom, I was trying to warn you when I asked you if you think you had a good lawyer."

The Warning from My Dream to My Mother

On November 23, my mother told me that she had applied for a job as a supervisor, and she felt that she would get the job because she was already doing the job. When my mother told me that, a whisper came to my ear to tell me that she would not be getting the supervisor job, but I didn't know how to tell her. I told my mother to just apply for another job. The job closed on December 25, and my mother did not get the job.

On September 03, 2007, I dreamt that my mother was going to have an accident; she was going to hit a truck, but she was going to be all right. I told her that it would be raining on that day. My mother said, "Josh, I have never hit a car or truck before." But I told my mom that she would be okay. On that Friday, my mother hit an AT&T telephone truck coming down the hill while it was raining. She was fine; she didn't get hurt.

My neighbor and I went to a hockey game, and I told my neighbor that I had a feeling somebody was going to break his stick. During the second half of the game, one of the players broke his hockey stick. Then a whisper came to my ear again that another player was going to break his hockey stick, and it happened.

Keeping the Faith in God

I believe that there are many of God's children out there that have the same belief and gift that I have. Stay true to yourself and always put the Lord Jesus Christ in your heart; he will always be there for you.

I don't know how this gift works or who gets to be chosen to have it. But I am glad that I have someone guiding my life other than my mother. My mother would always tell me about her dreams and ask me what I thought. I always told her that they could mean two things. My mother said, "Joshua, I think you have the gift of analyzing my dreams." Whatever that means, I have accepted God as my savior, and without him I would not be able to have the faith and the knowledge to believe in my dreams or his whispers in my ear that help me stay focused.

My Mom said according to Oprah, "Everyone is instinctive, (some more than others) and you should pay more attention to it."

Printed in the United States
by Baker & Taylor Publisher Services